In Our Backyard

Written & Illustrated
by
Geoffrey Kenneth Jenson

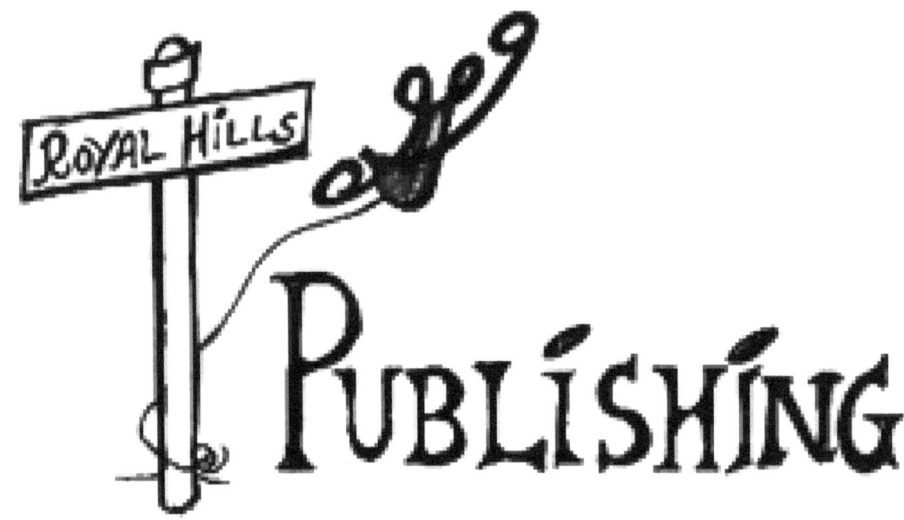

Dedicated to,
Mama and Dad.

In Our Backyard

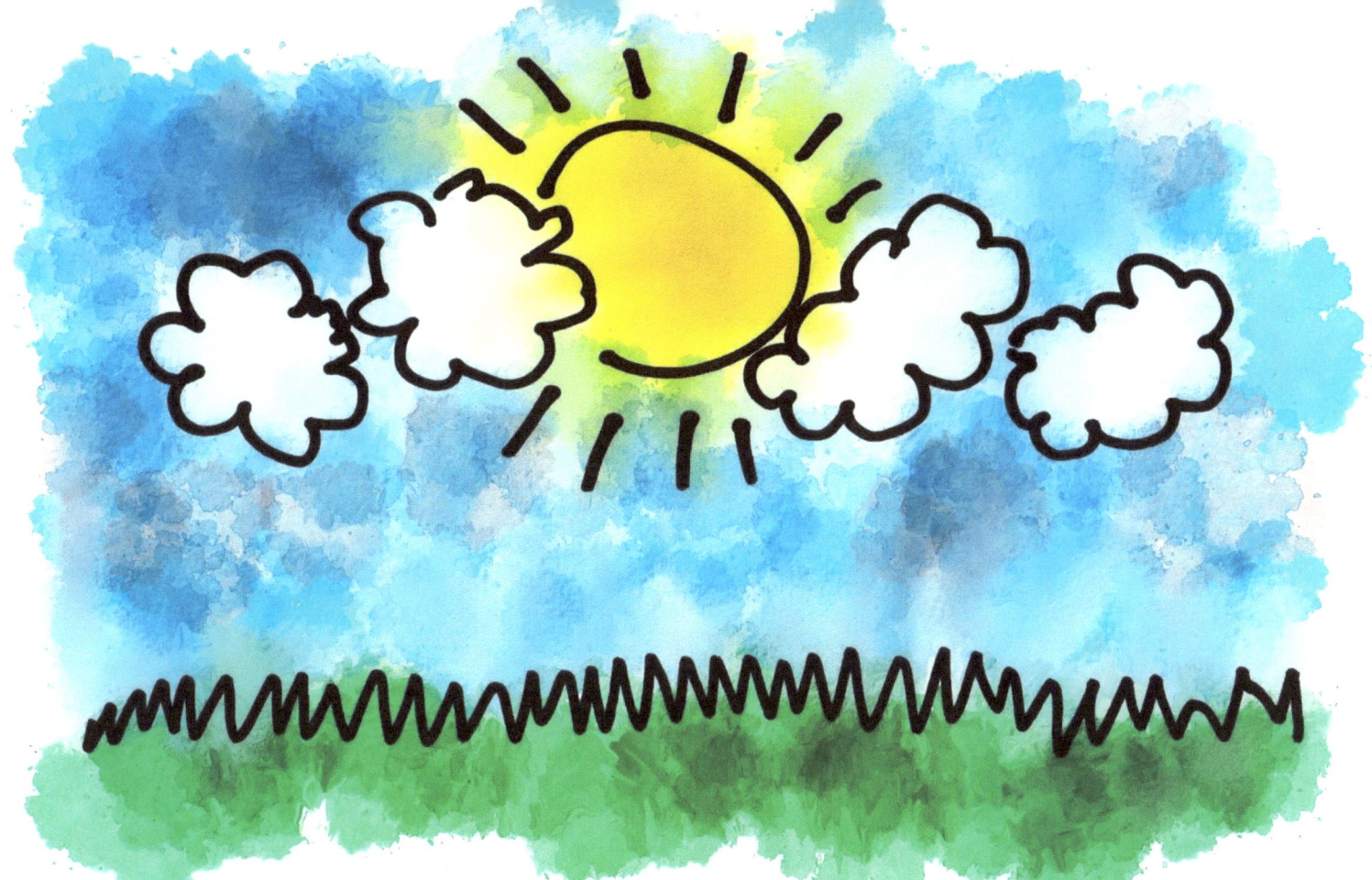

In our backyard, there is a big field of green grass, a bright sun, and a sky with clouds that changes colors.

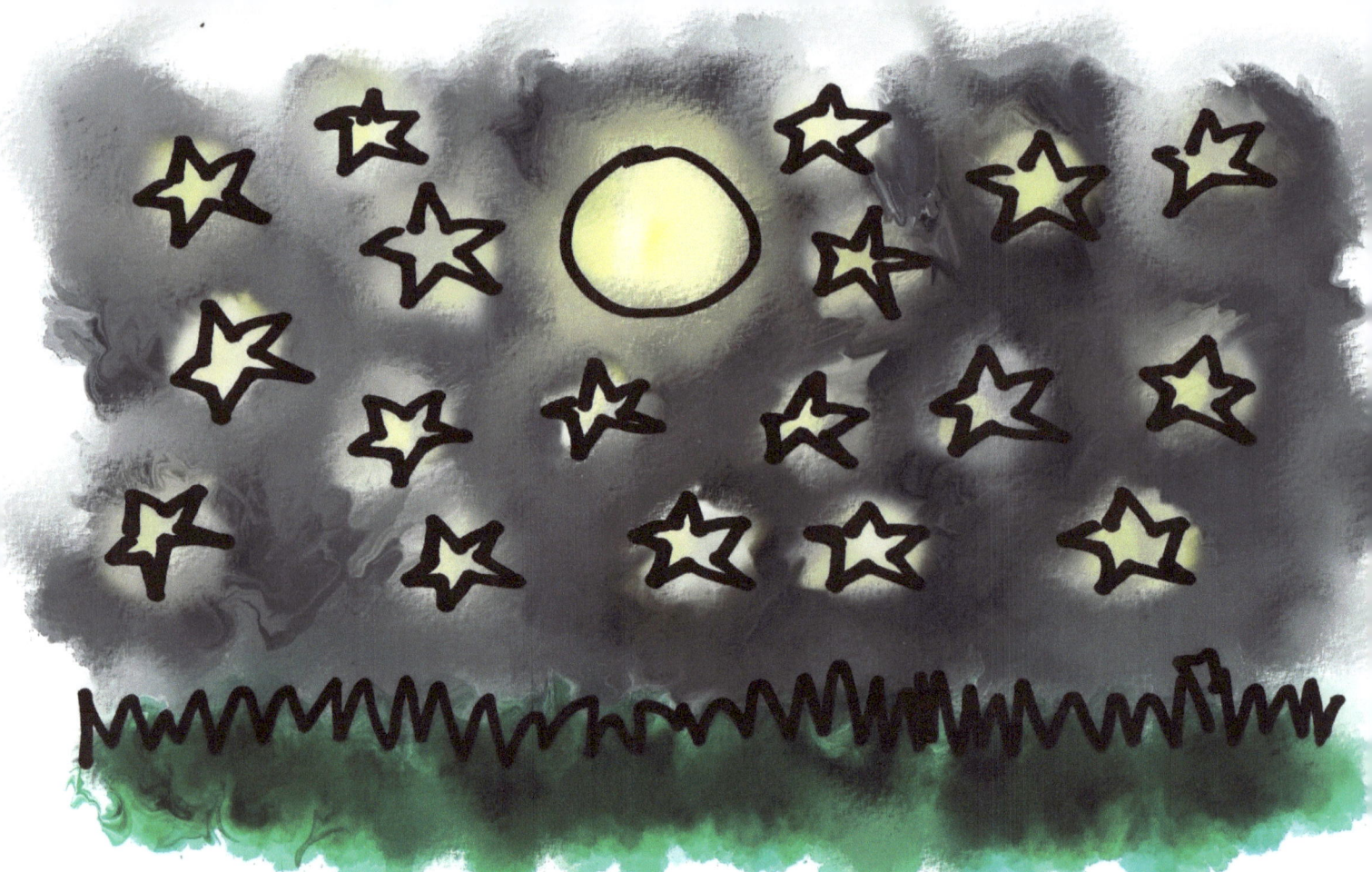

After the sun goes down,
a big moon with many little,
shiny star friends appears where
the sun once was.

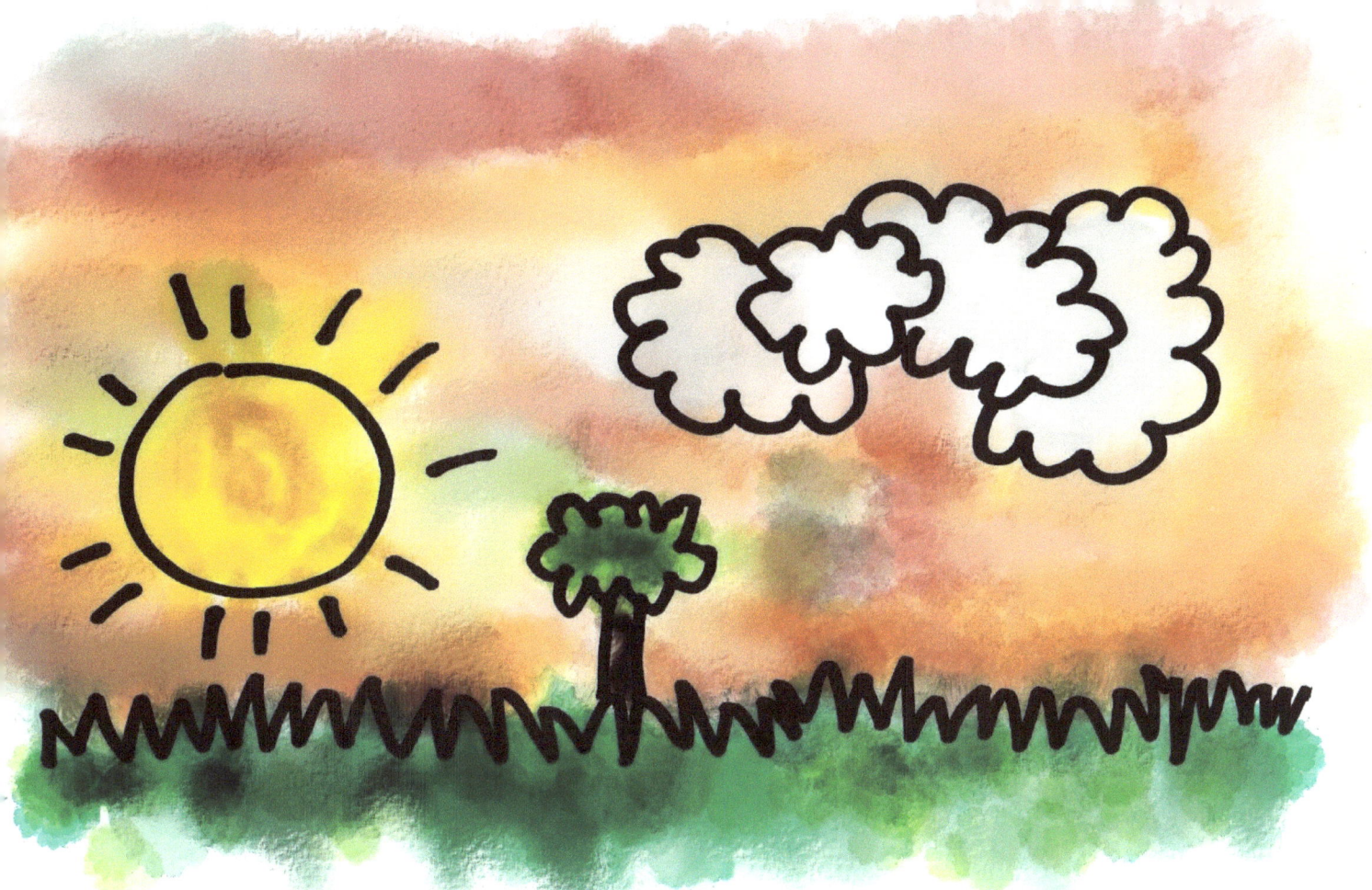

One morning,
we planted a small tree.

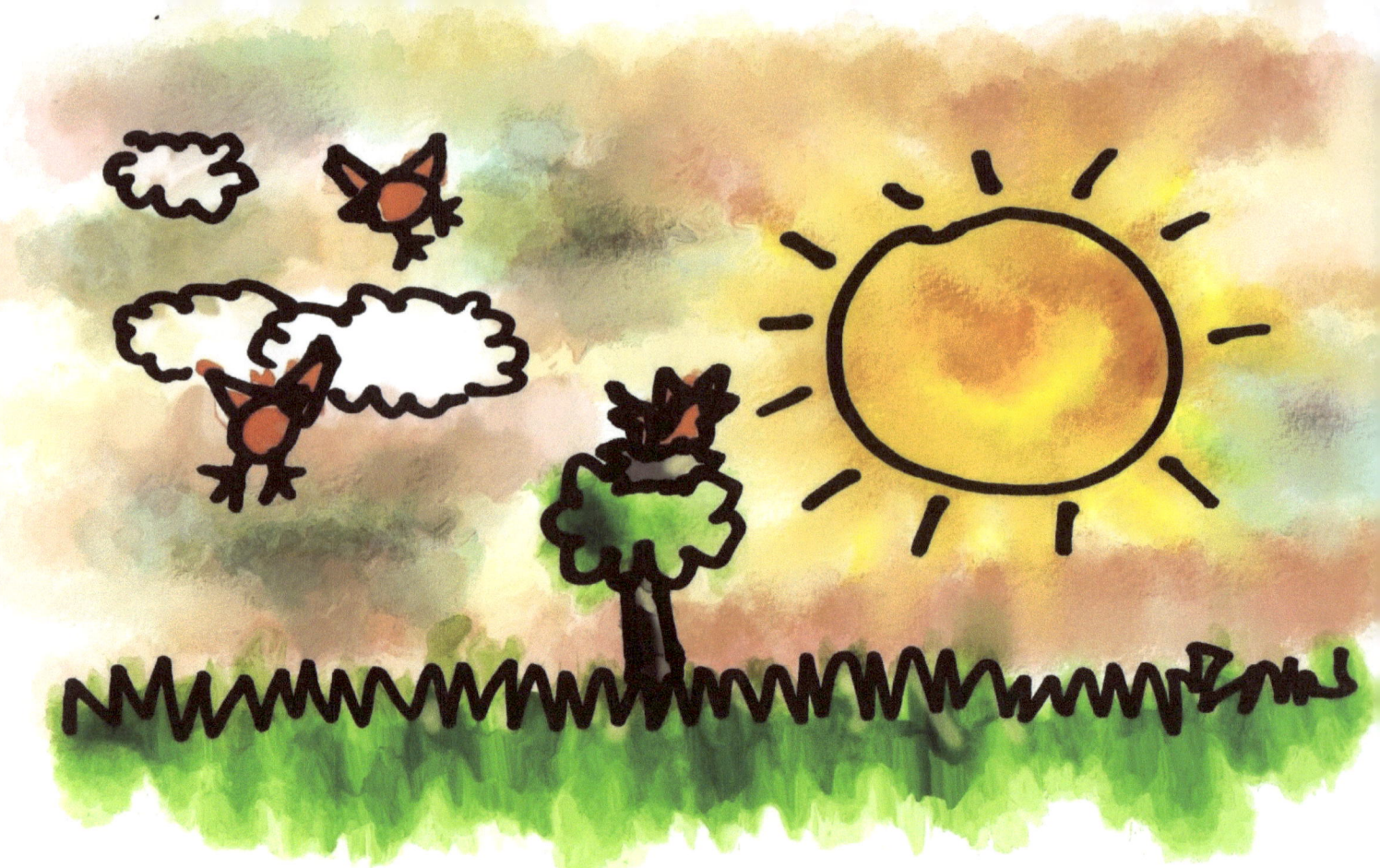

After we planted the small tree, many birds came. They even made a small nest at the top of the tree!

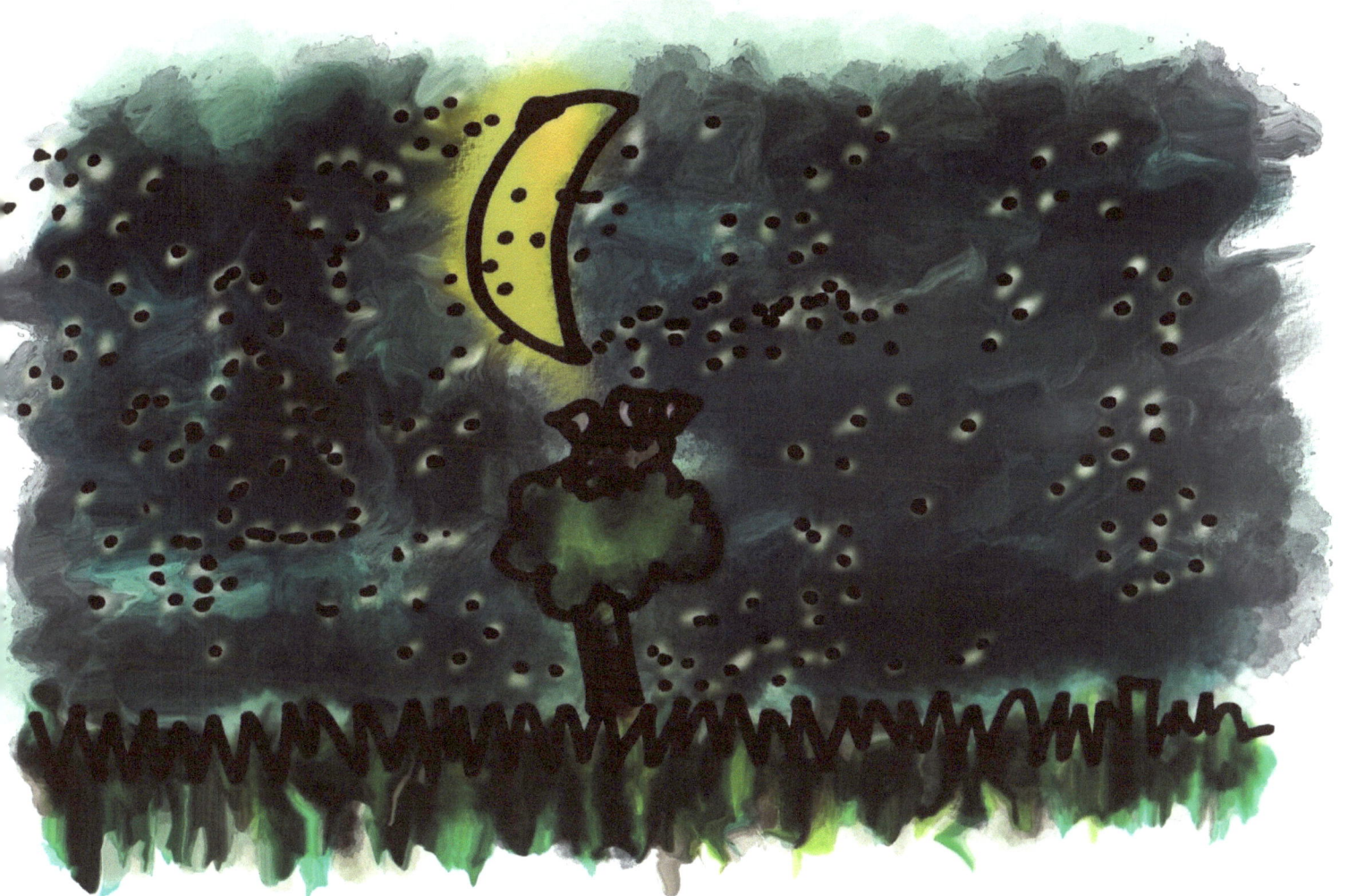

I love watching the birds but the fireflies at night are my favorite.

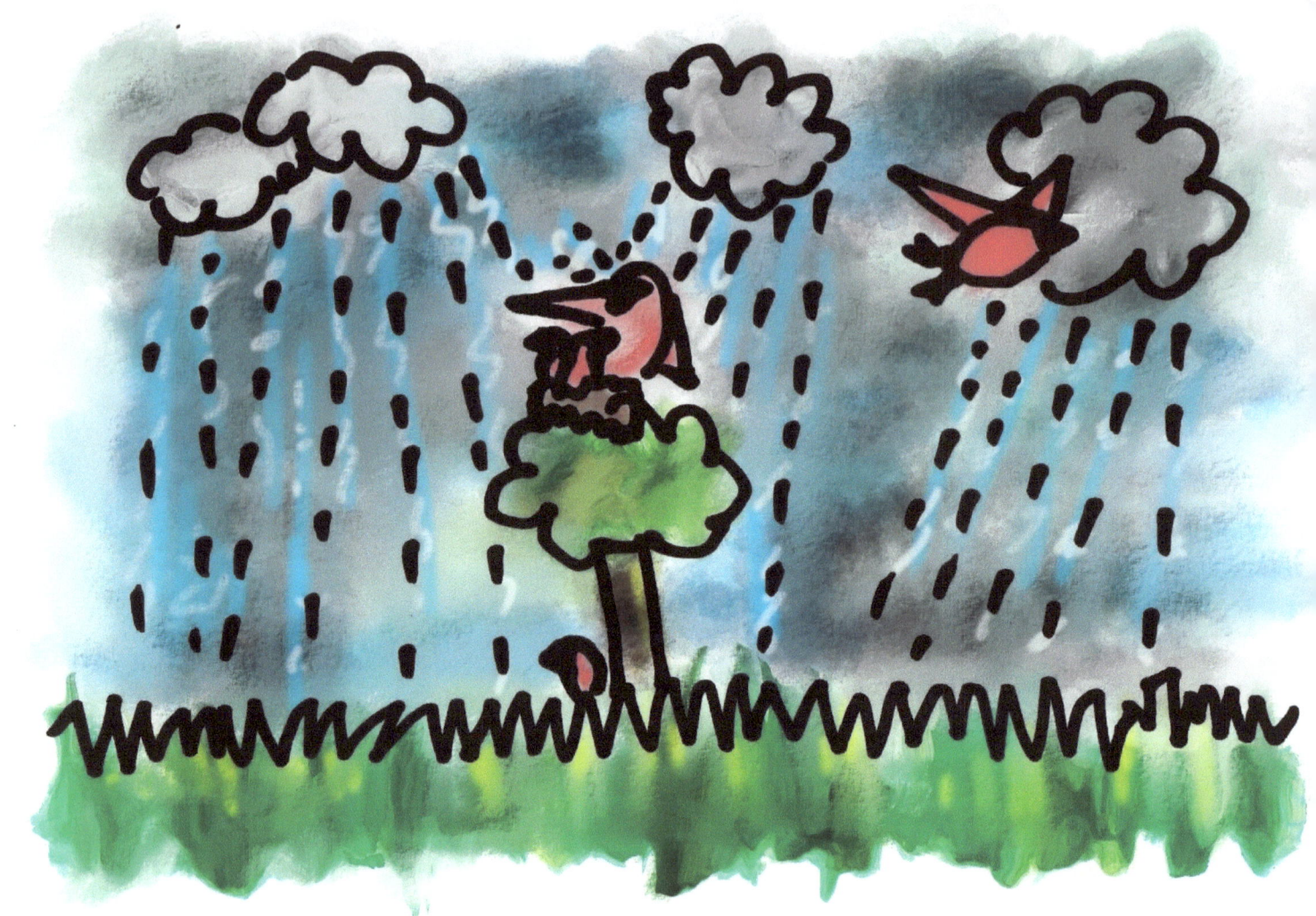

In our backyard,
it rained a little...

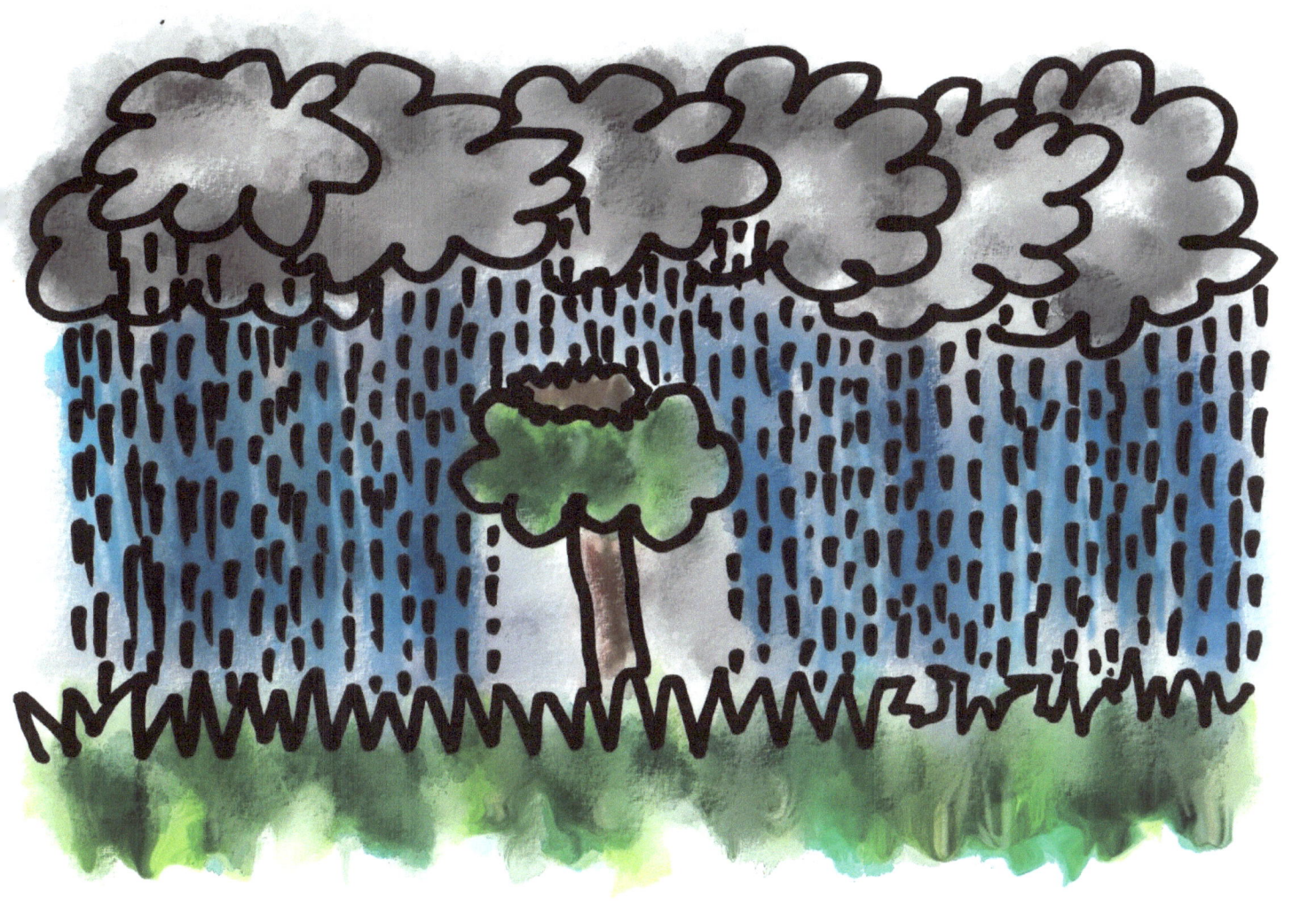

Then, it rained a lot!

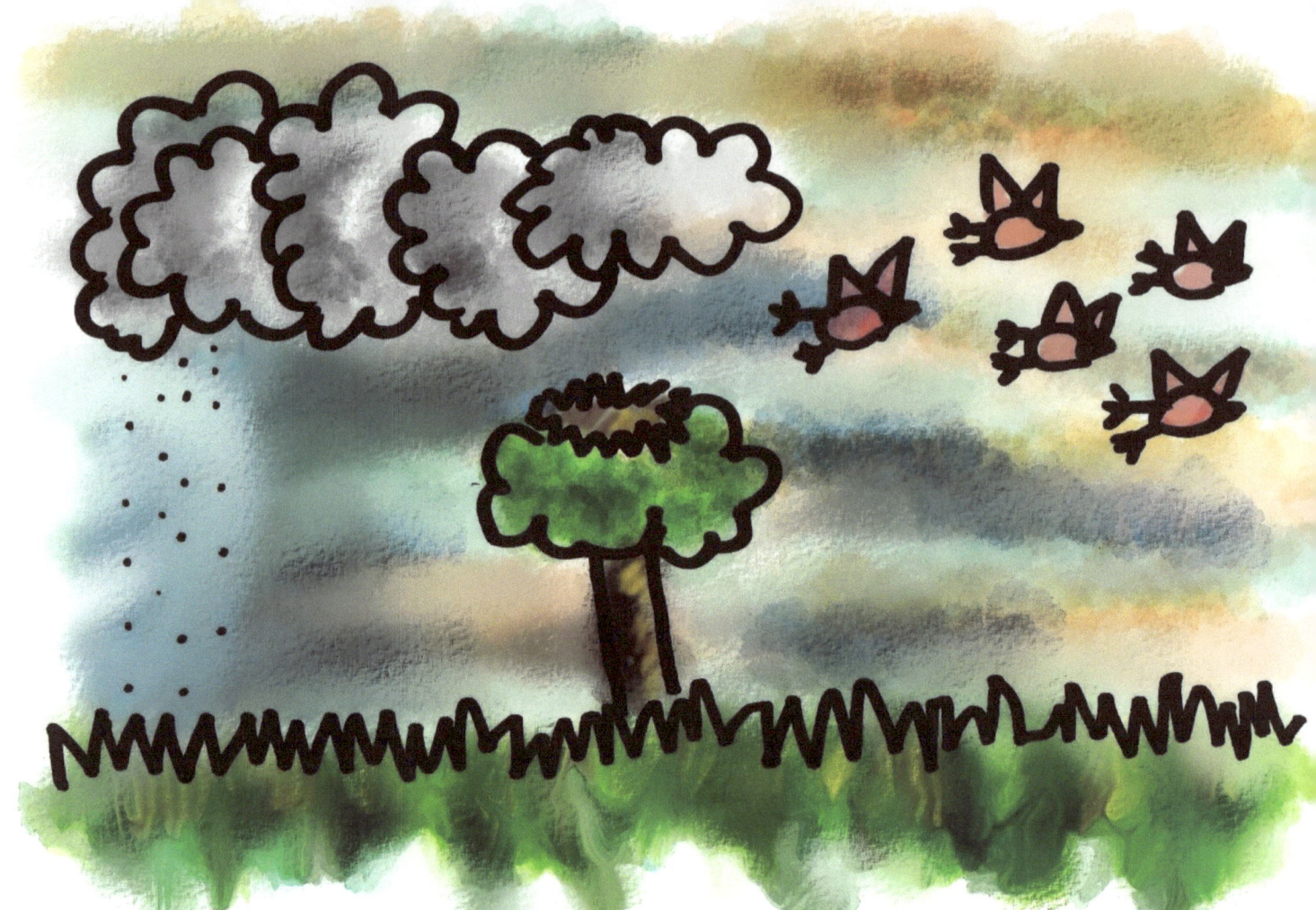

The birds didn't like the rain
because before it rained so much
they all flew away.

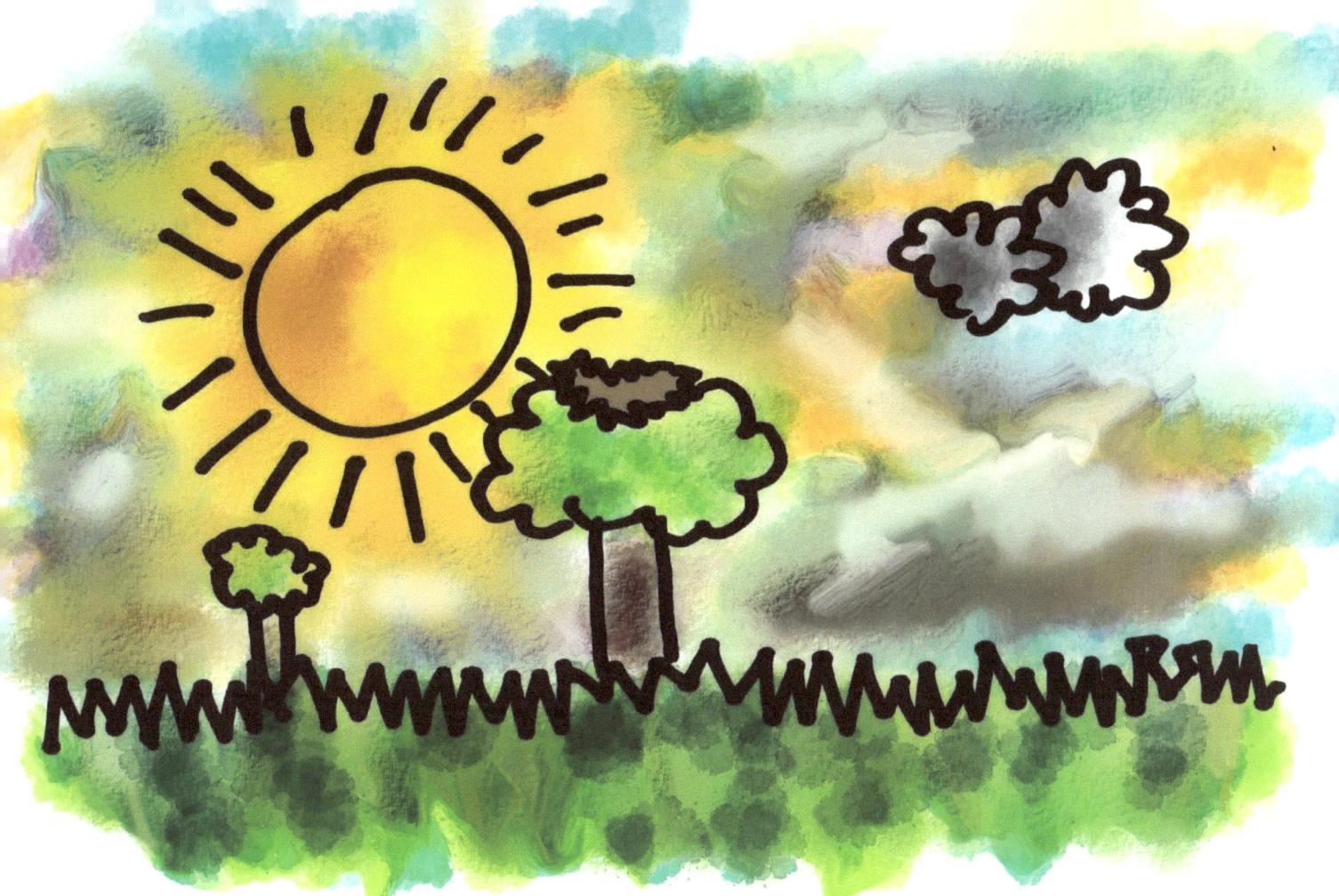

We thought our tree may get lonely without the birds. So, we planted another small tree beside it.

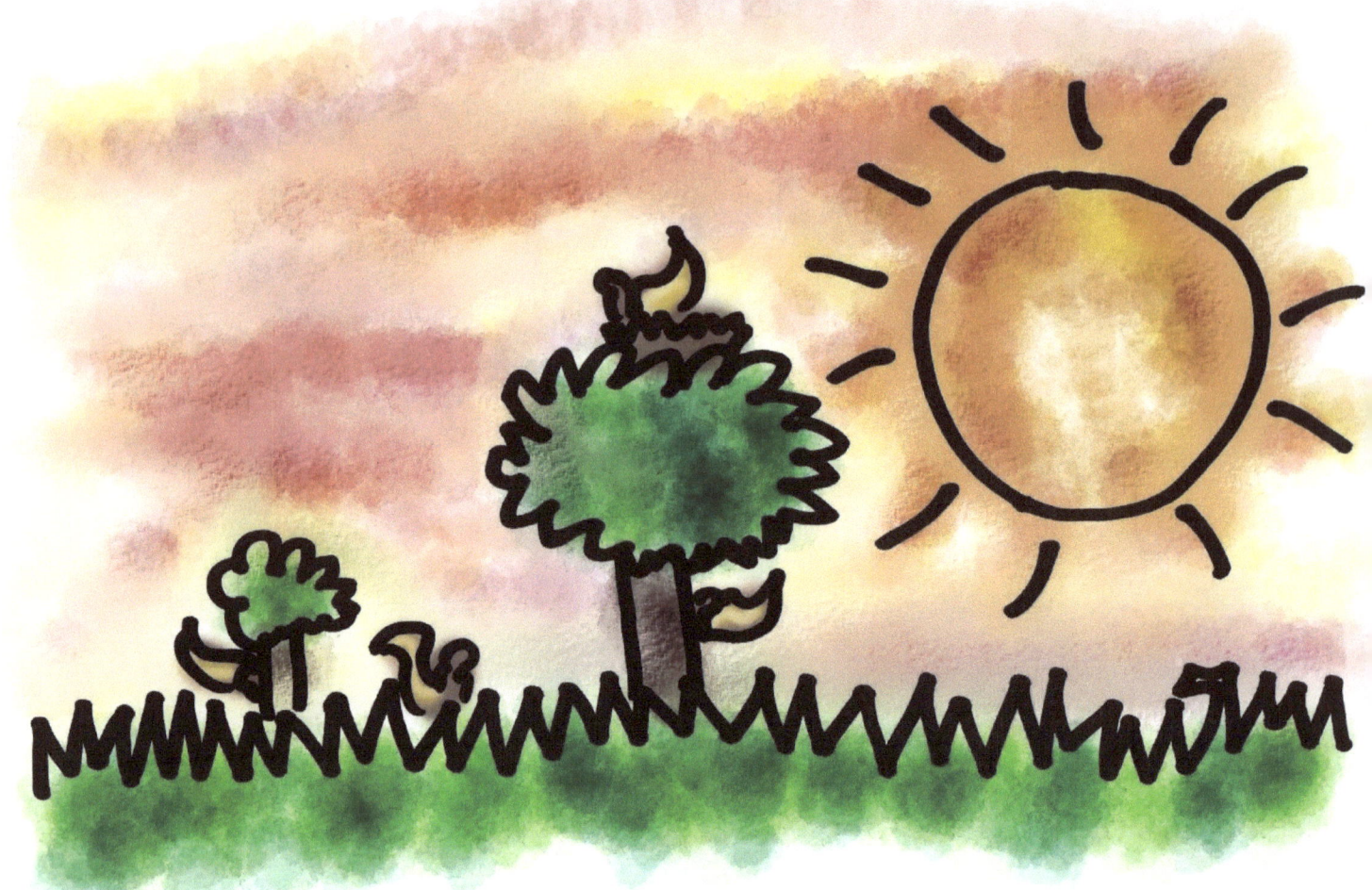

After we planted the small tree
many squirrels came. I love
watching them play hide and seek.

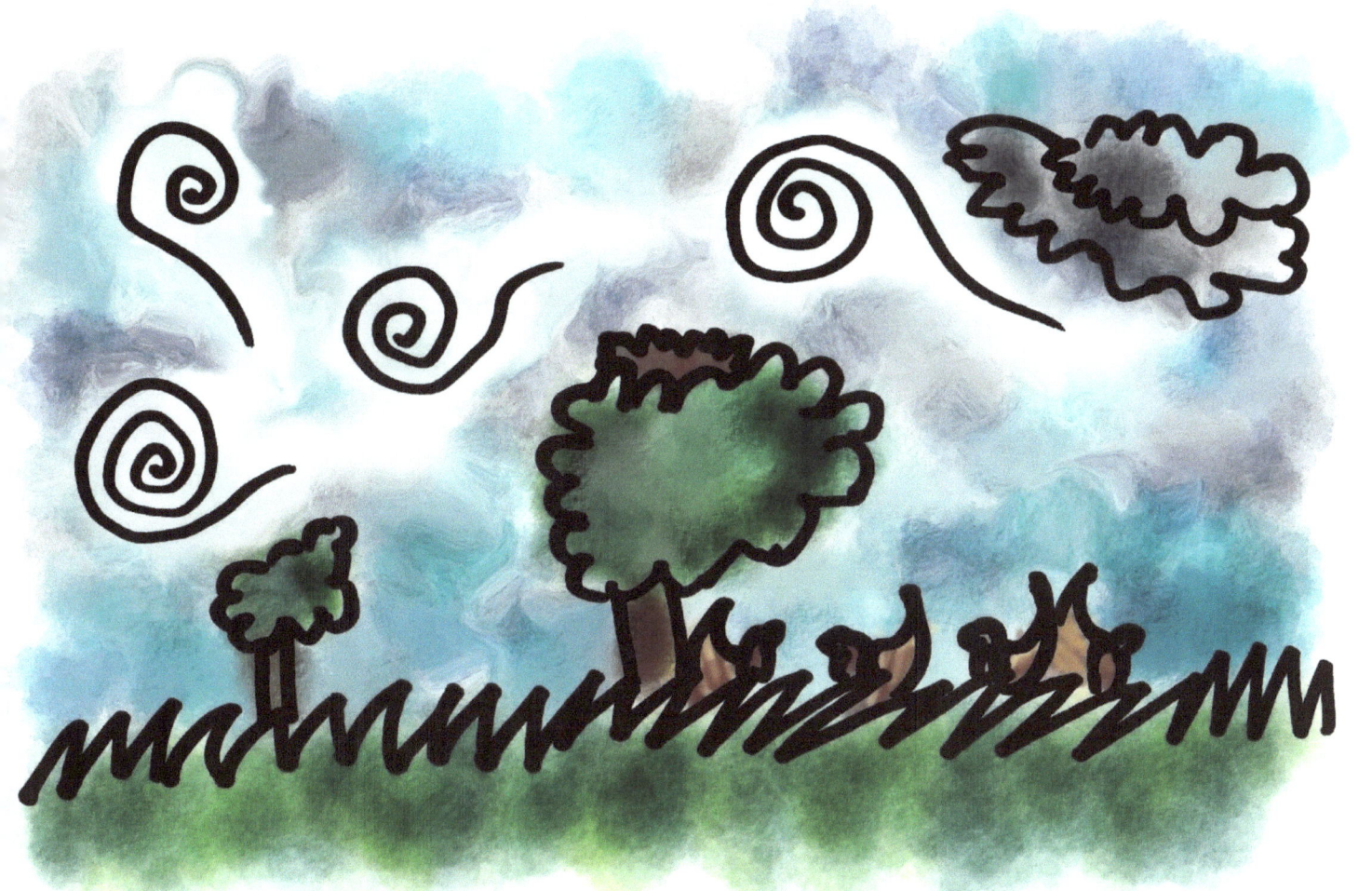

In our backyard,
it got windy...

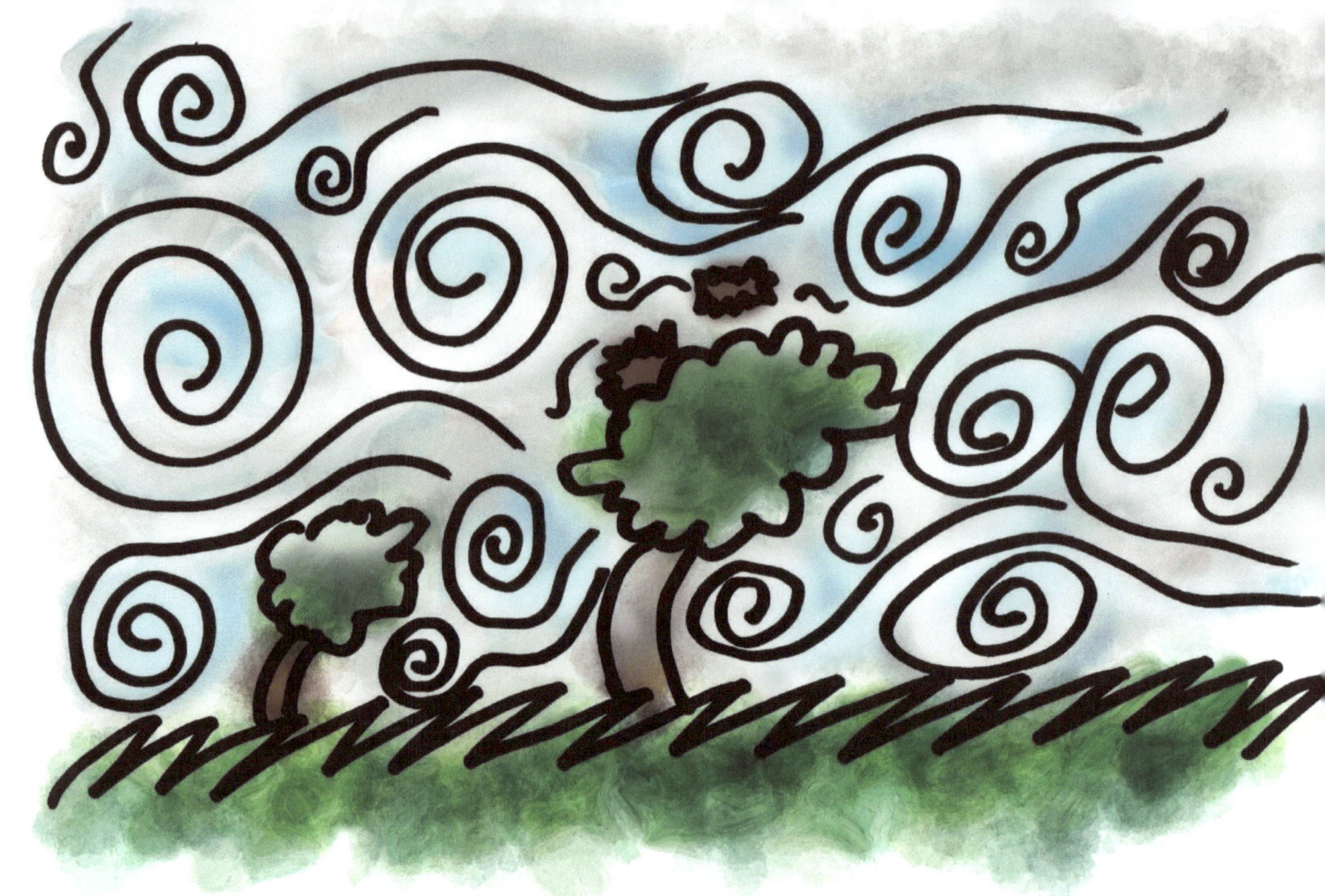

Then, it got very windy!

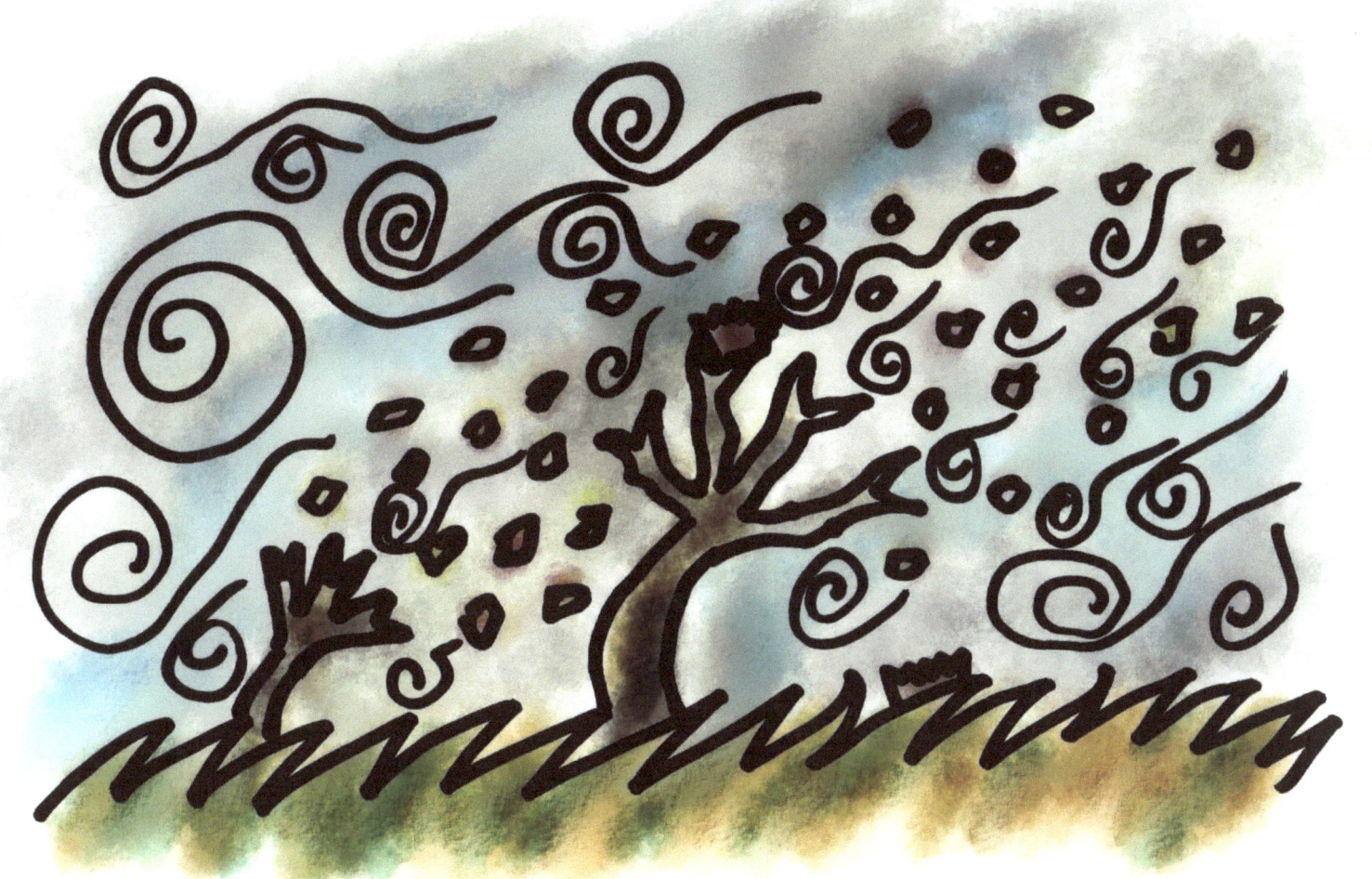

I think the squirrels didn't like
the wind because the wind blew
all the leaves off the trees.

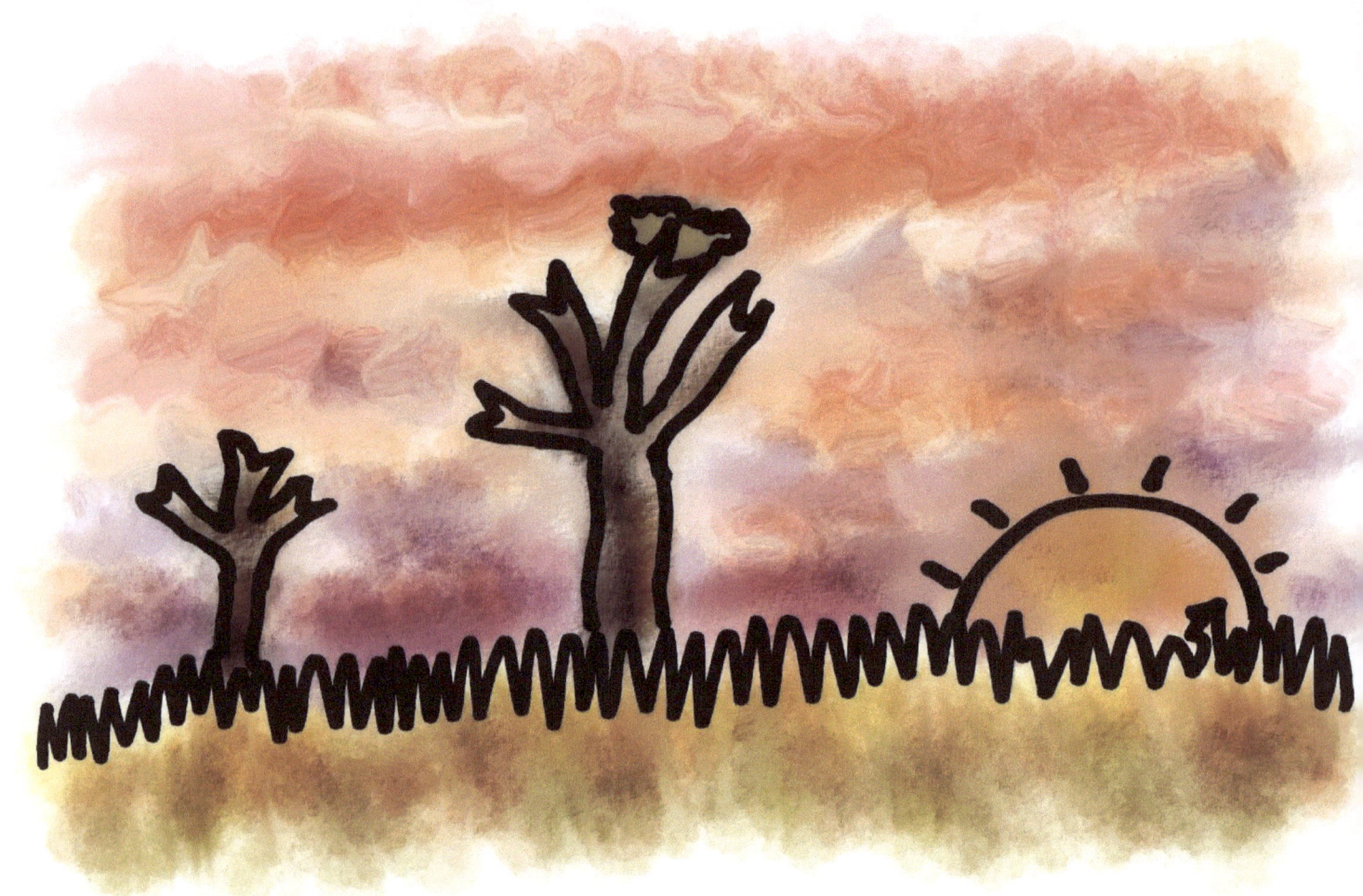

And after that,
I didn't see the squirrels anymore.

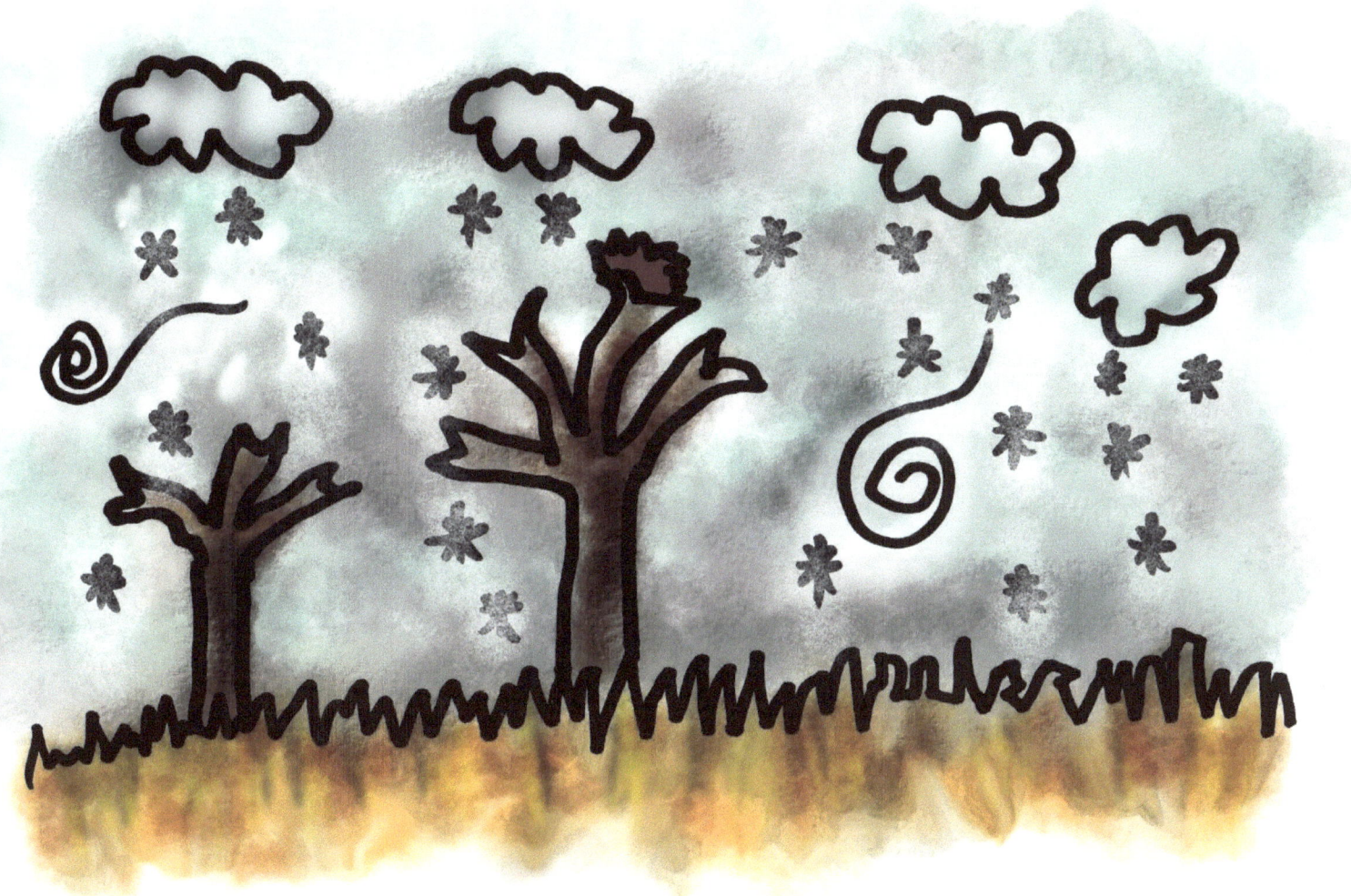

In our backyard,
it snowed a little.

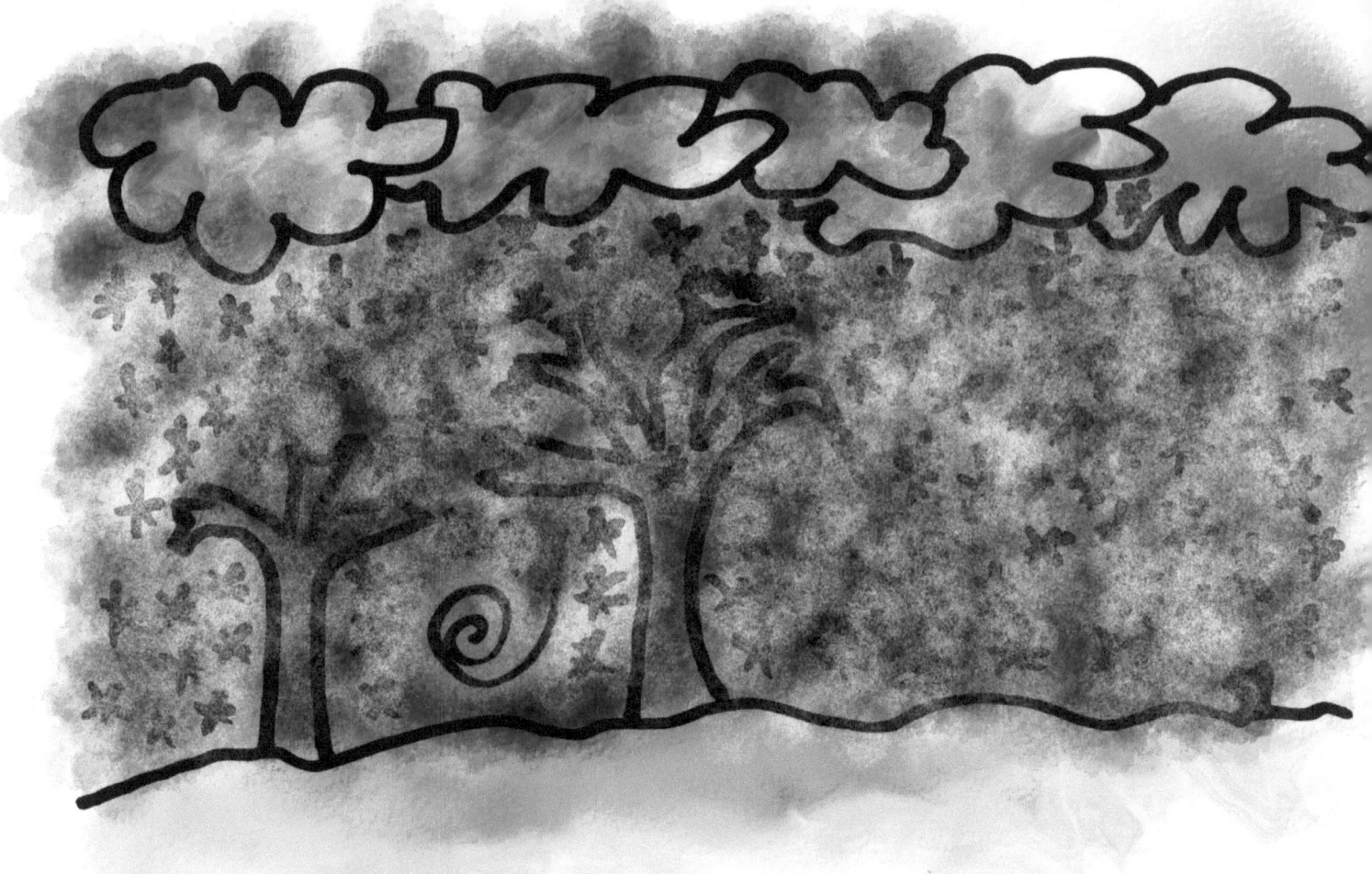

Then, it snowed a lot!

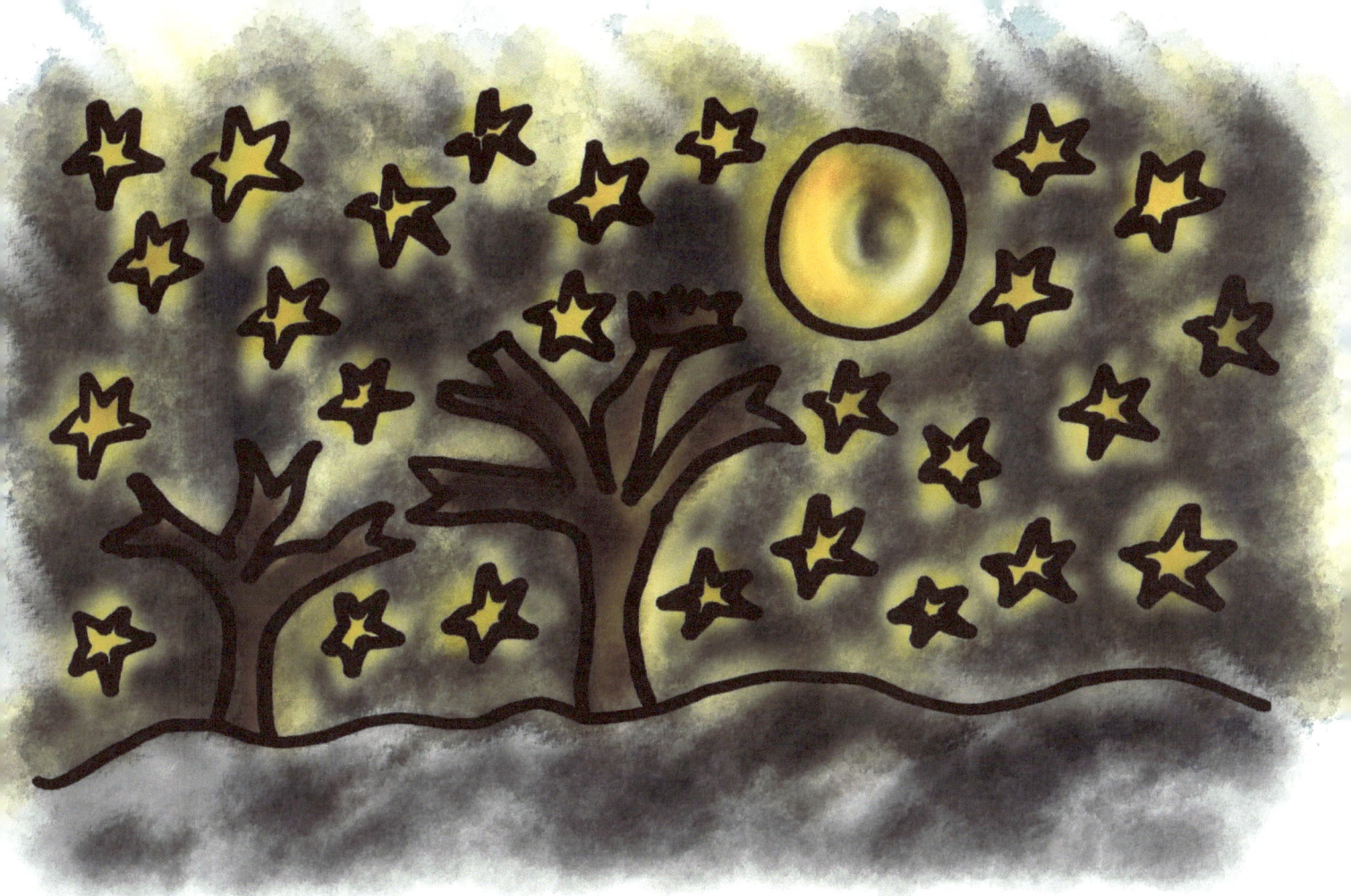

After the snow stopped falling,
the moon and its star friends
shined the brightest.

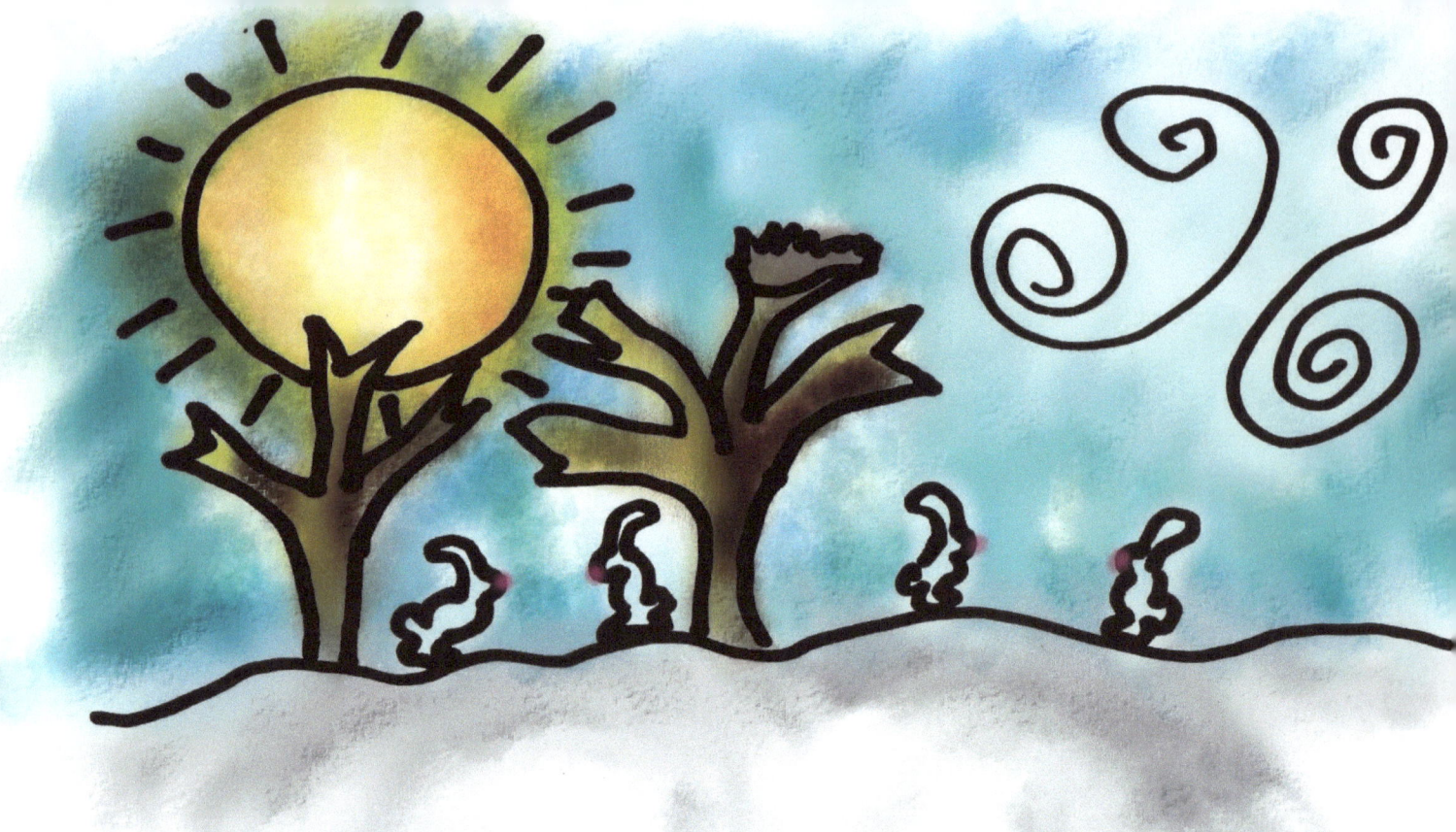

I know the squirrels didn't like
the snow but the rabbits
they sure do!

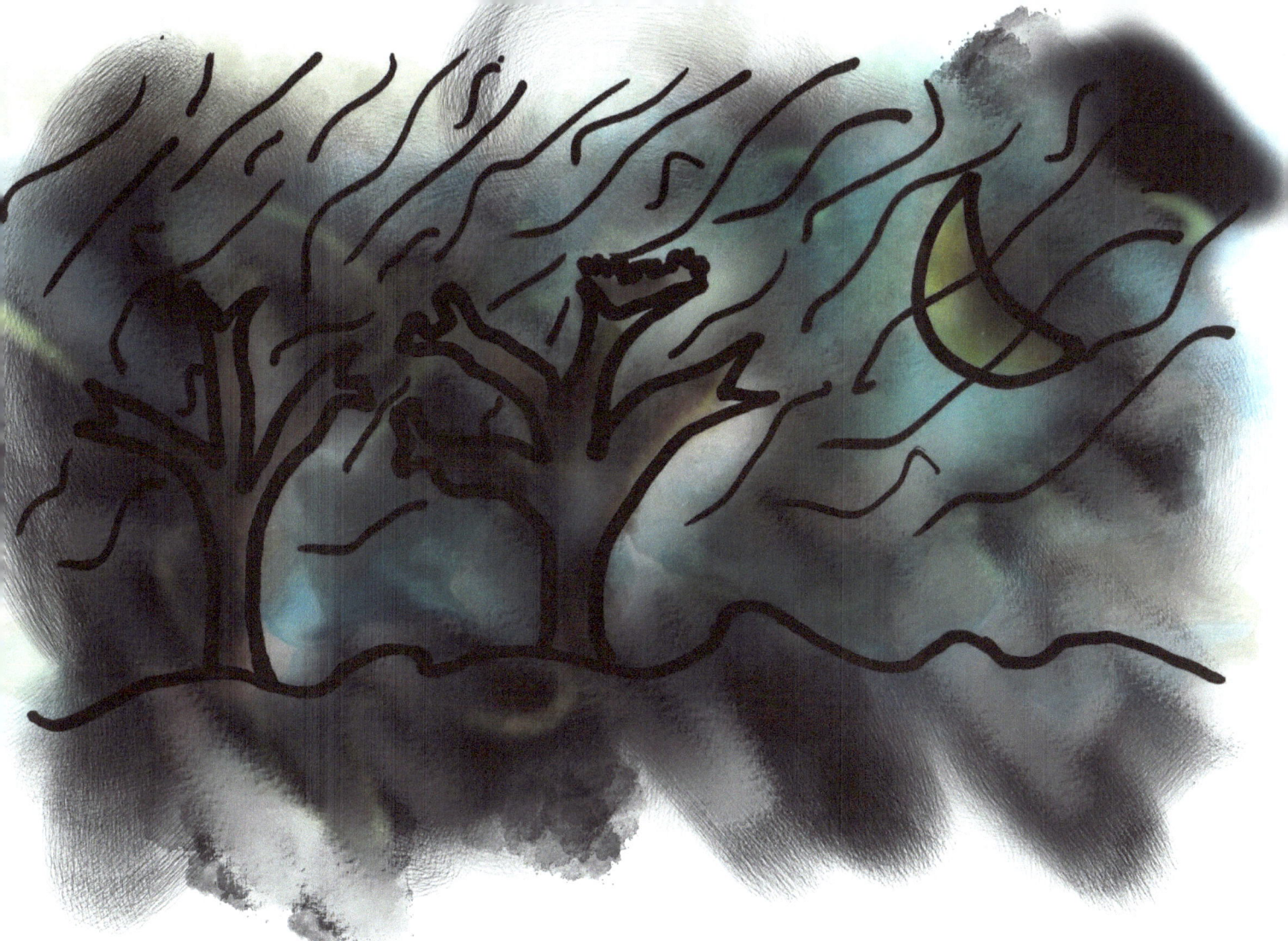

One night, there were
strange pretty lights glowing
in the sky.

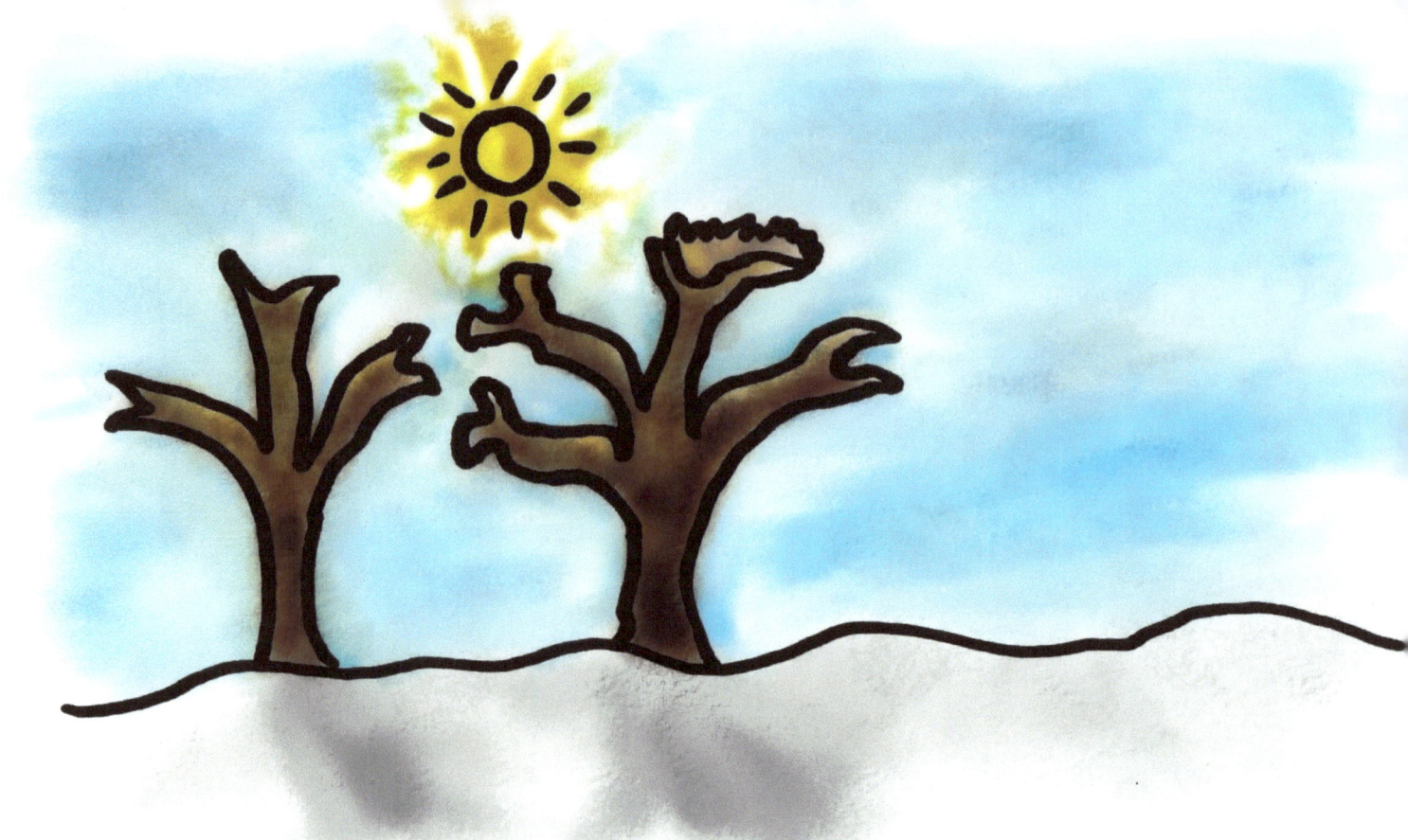

In our backyard,
the sun came back
and climbed in the sky.

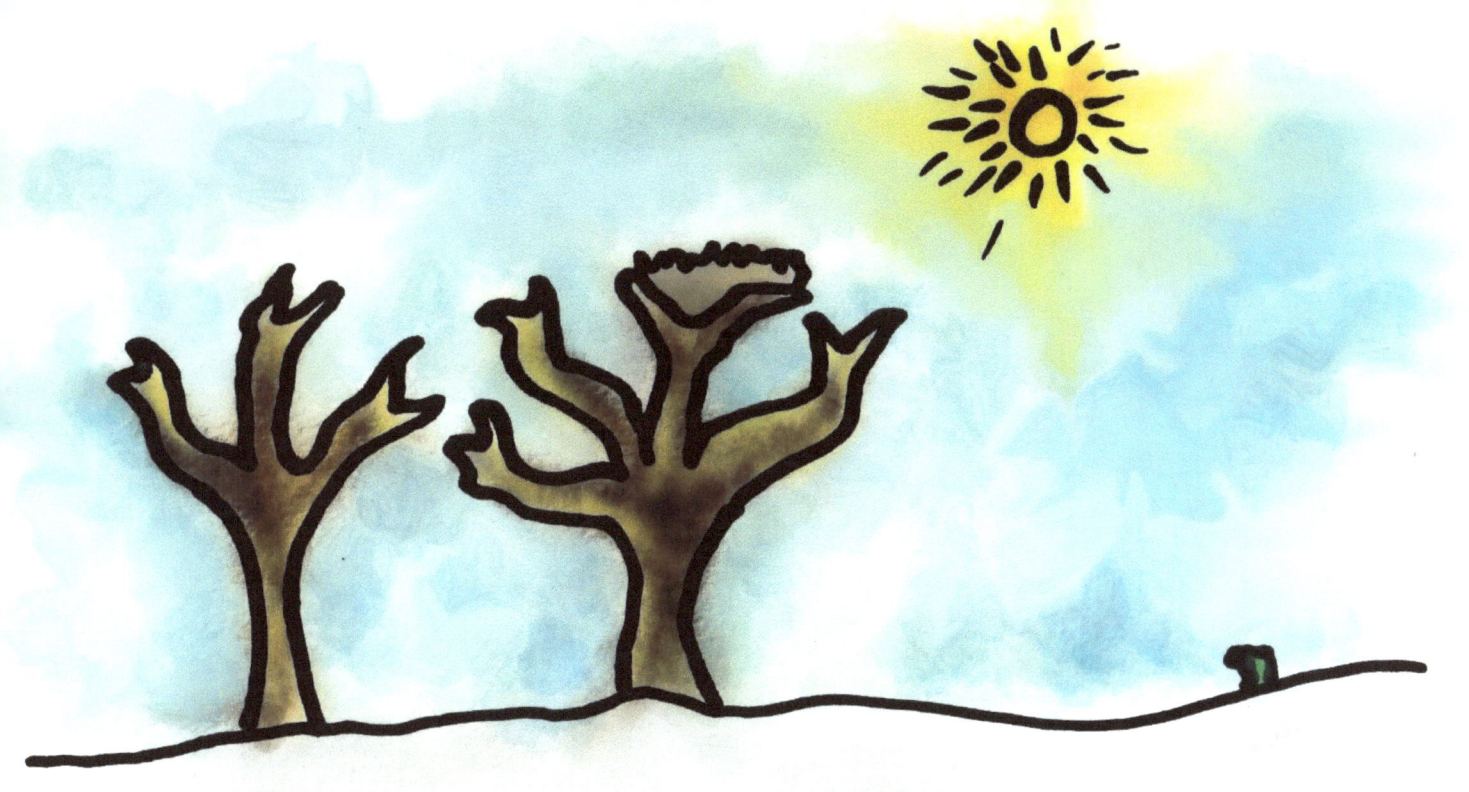

Then, it climbed really high!

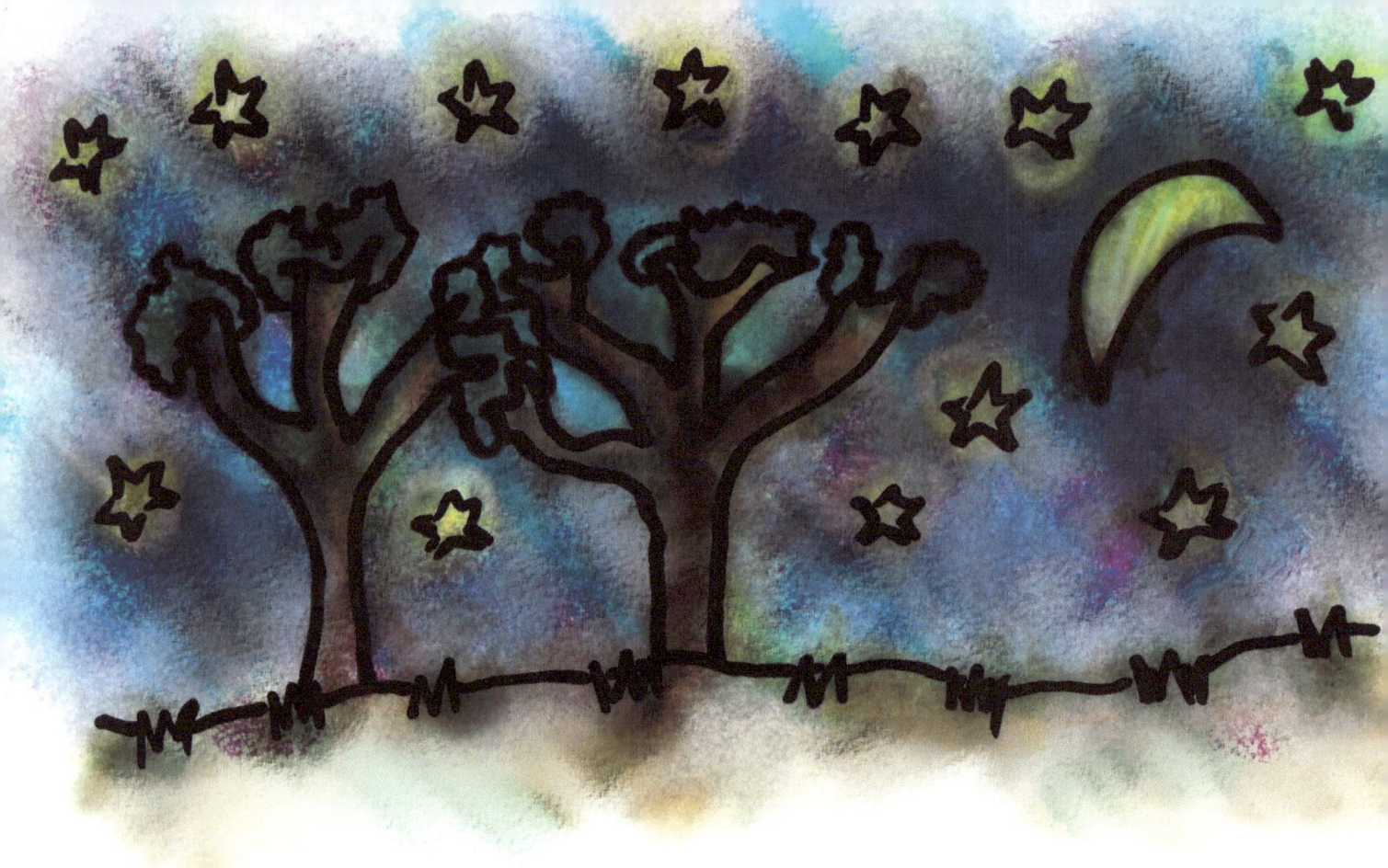

Little by little the
snow melted away.

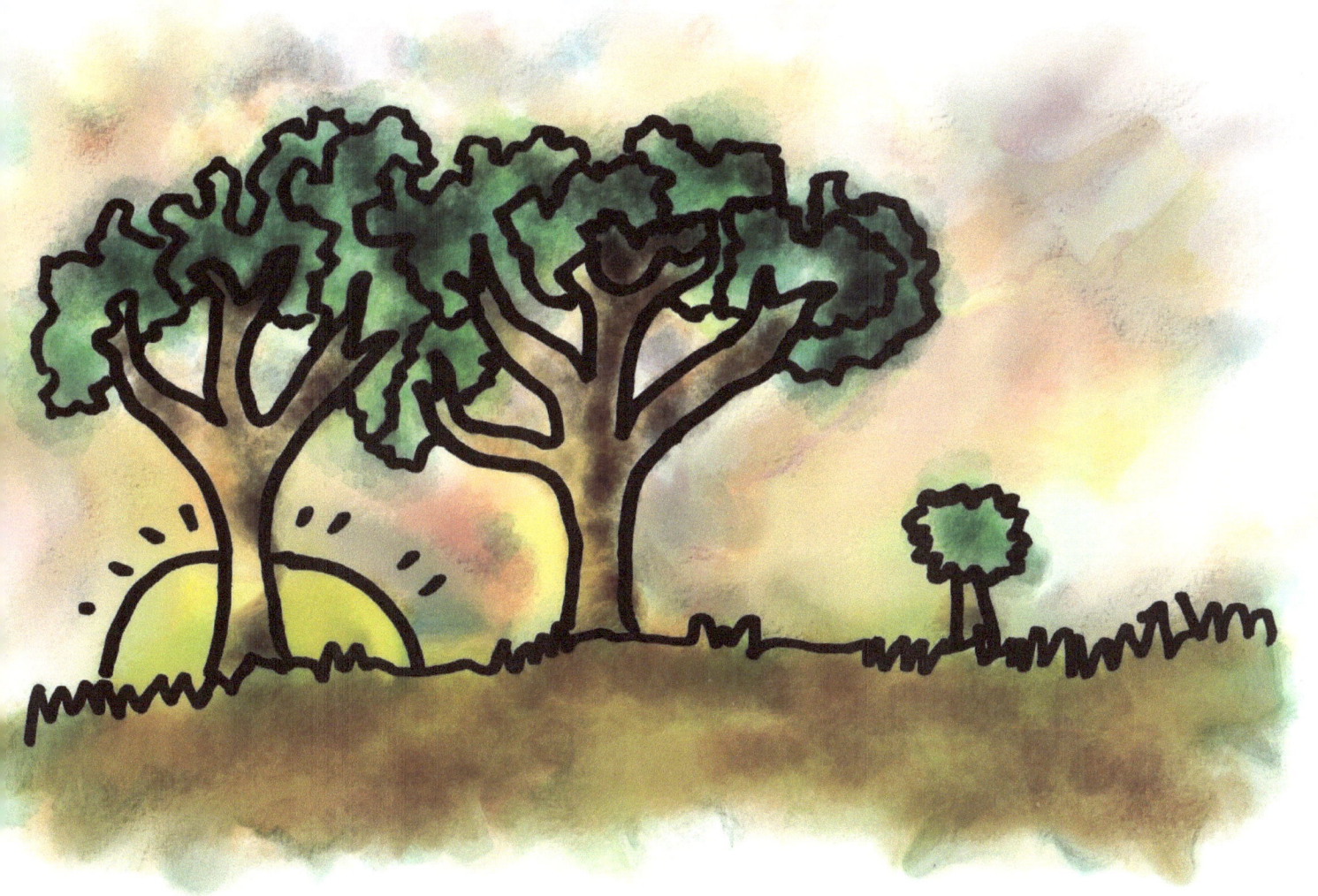

One morning,
we planted our last small tree.

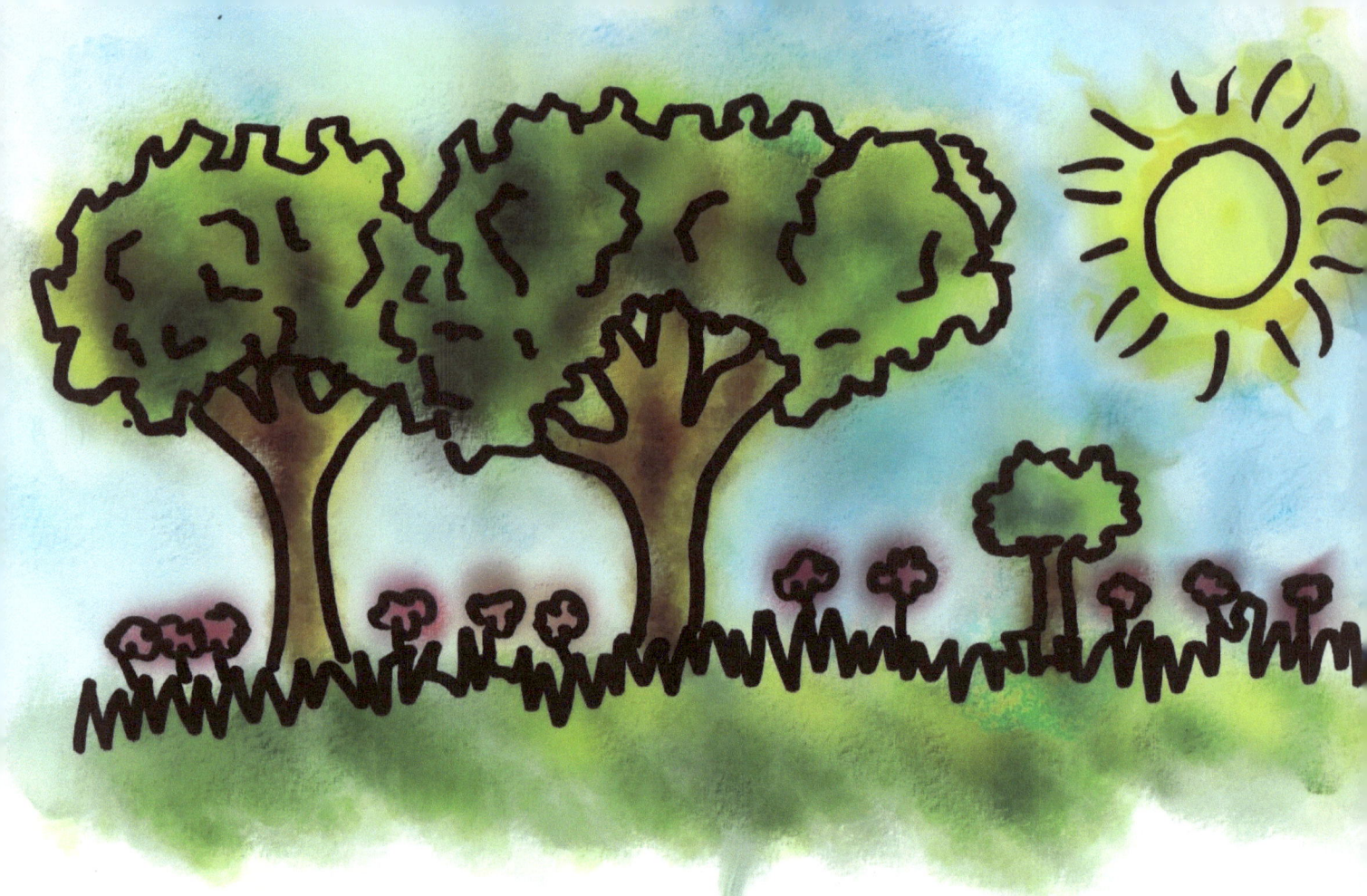

After we planted the small tree,
the grass turned green,
the trees' leaves grew back,
and flowers popped up everywhere

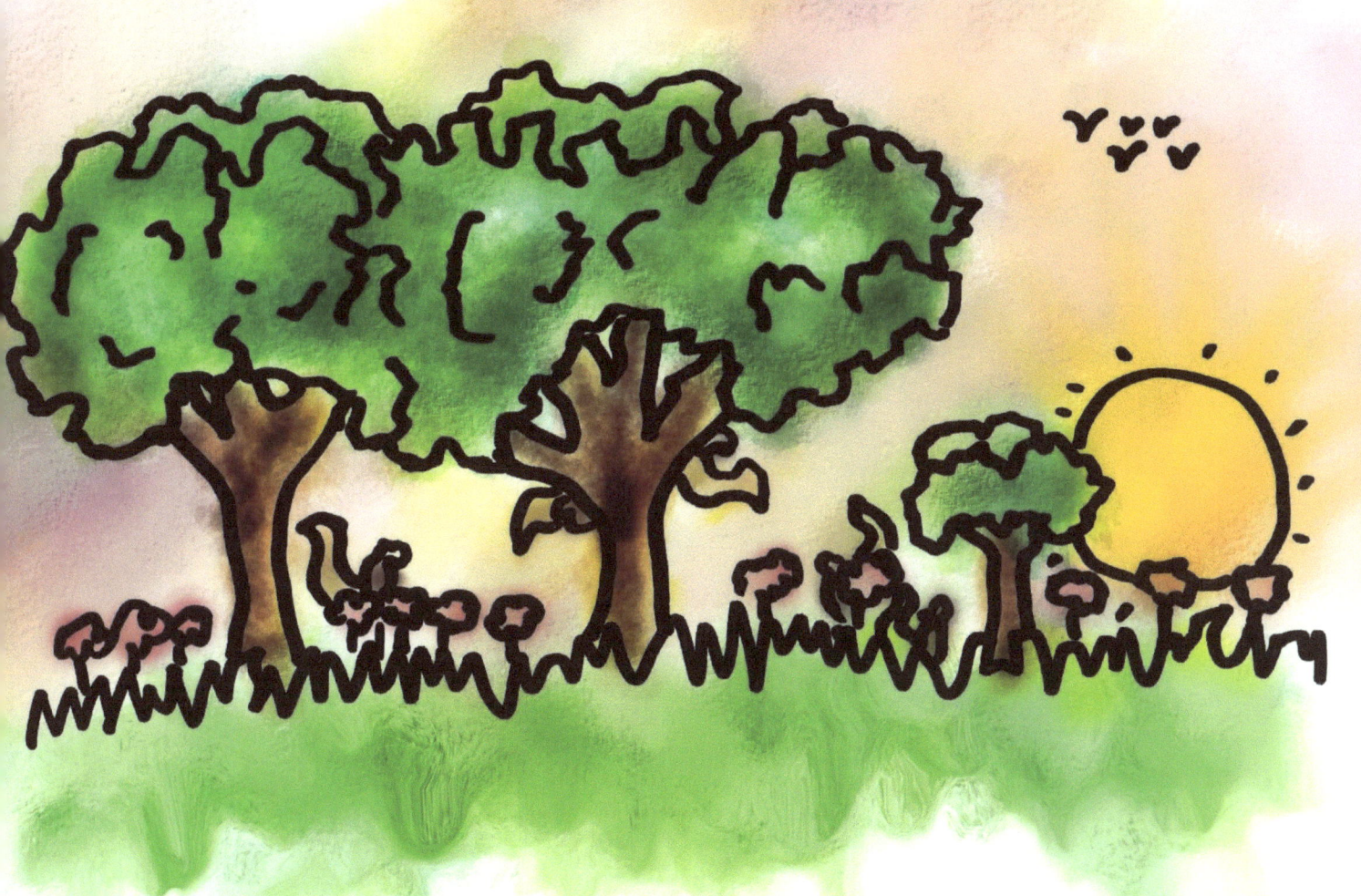

I think the birds and the squirrels like the flowers because they came back too!

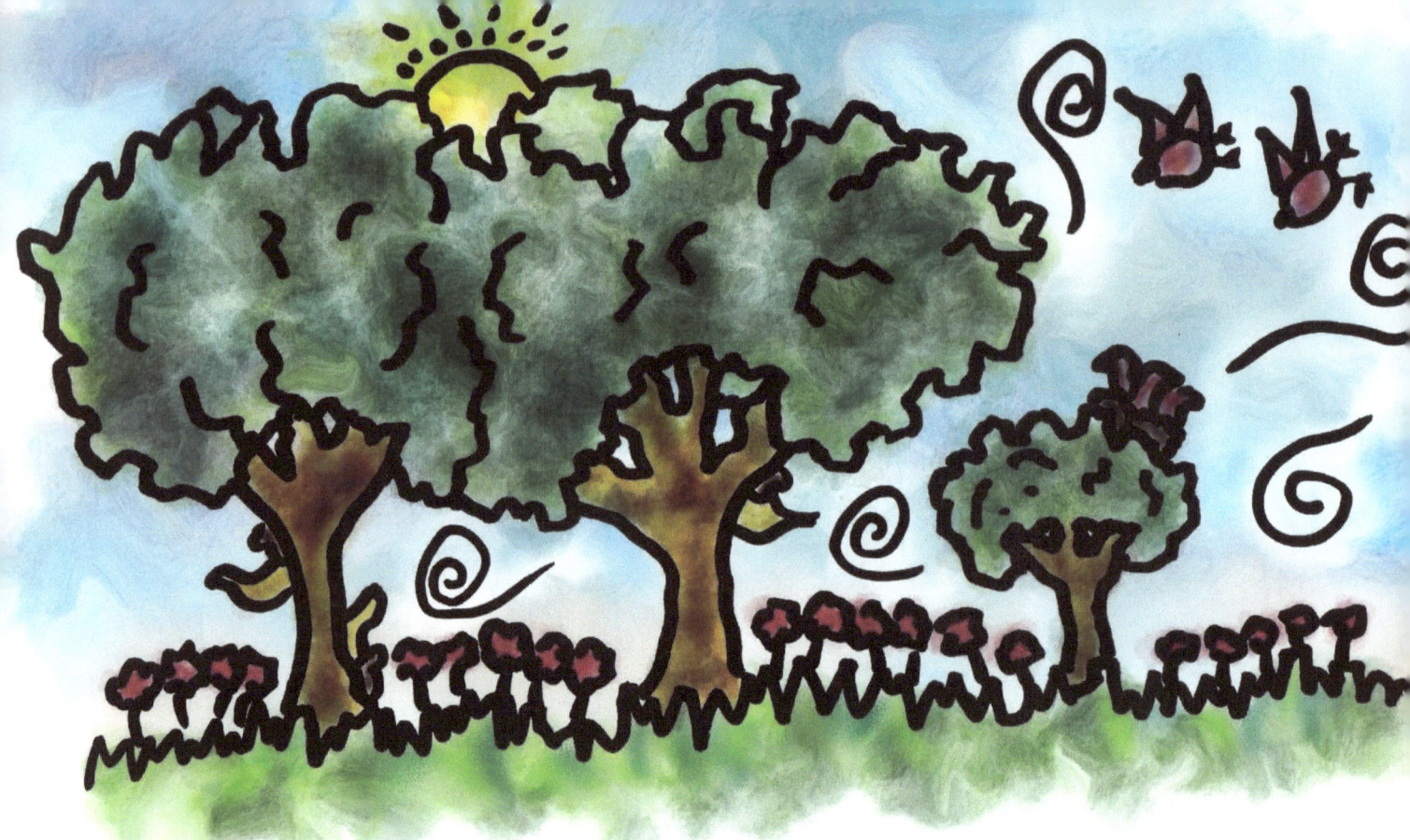

In our backyard,
there is a big field of green grass
with flowers everywhere.

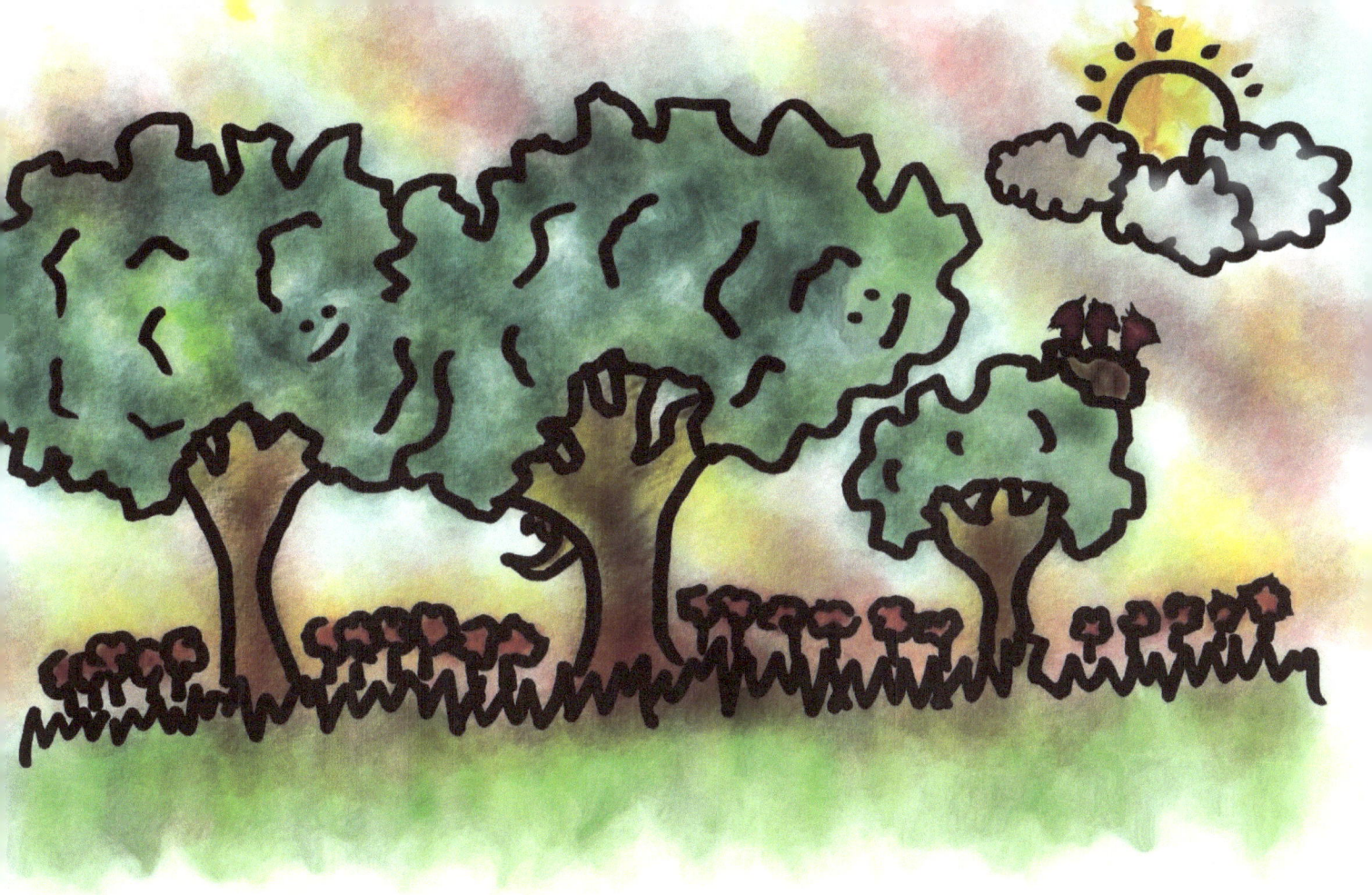

A bright sun in a sky with clouds
that changes colors.

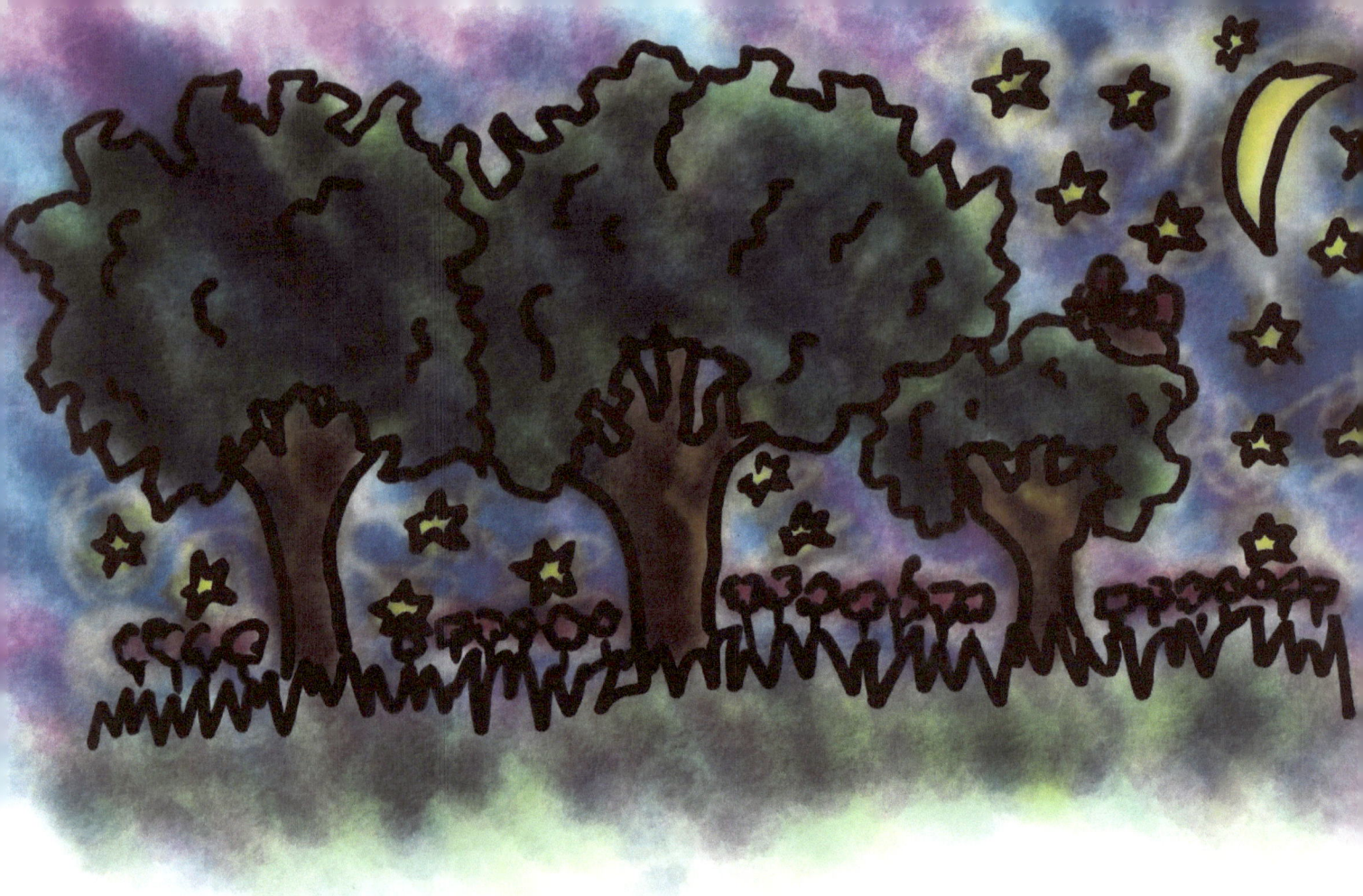

A moon with many little,
shiny star friends.

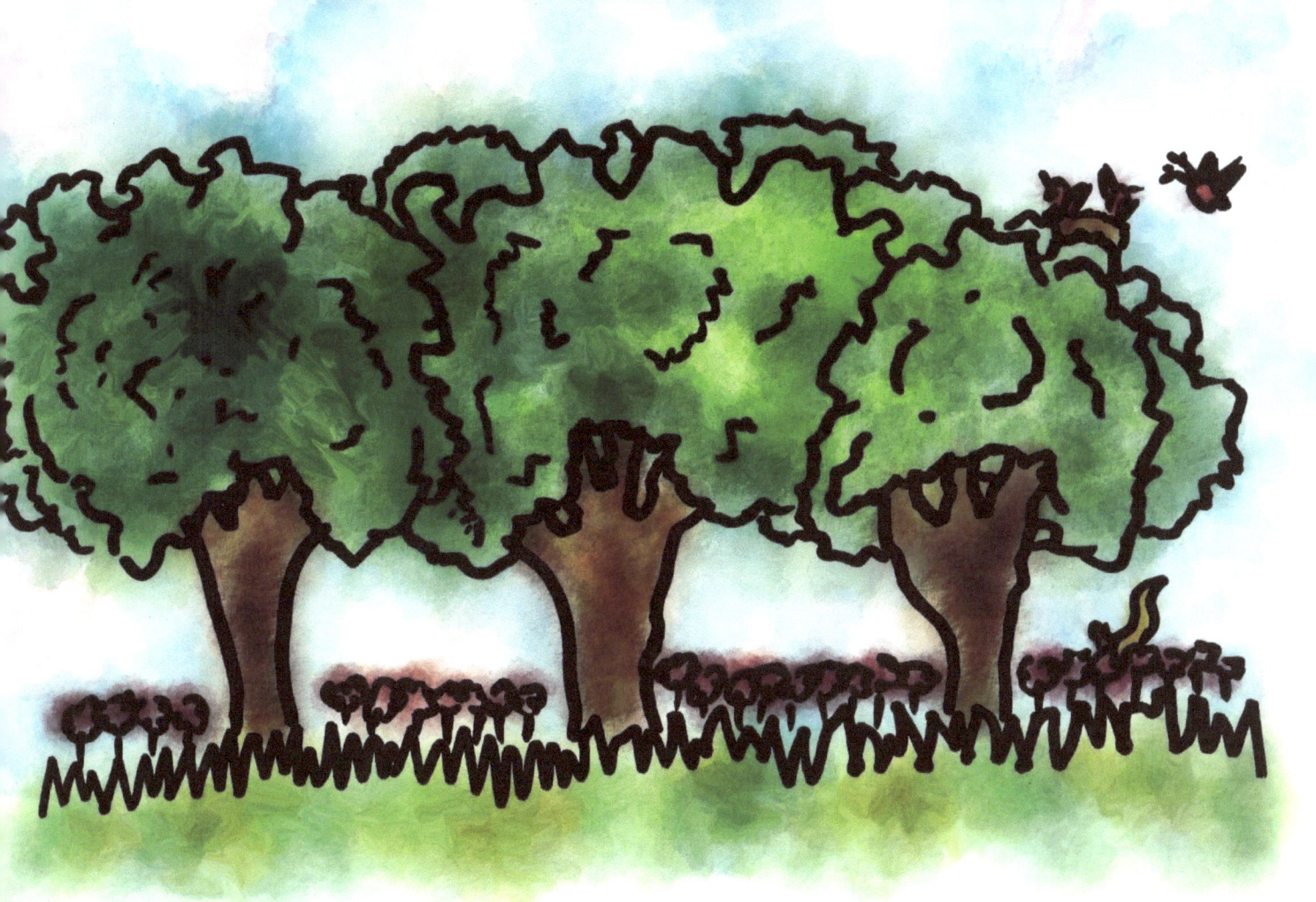

And three big trees...